Linda Tallent a

BOYS WILL BE
BRILLIANT!

How we can help get it right for boys in early years

Featherstone
An imprint of Bloomsbury Publishing Plc

50 Bedford Square   1385 Broadway
London   New York
WC1B 3DP   NY 10018
UK   USA

www.bloomsbury.com

Bloomsbury is a registered trademark of Bloomsbury Publishing Plc

First published 2016

© Linda Tallent and Gary Wilson, 2016

Photography © Shutterstock, © LEYF, © Acorn Childcare Ltd.

British Library Cataloguing-in-Publication Data
A catalogue record for this book is available from the British Library.

ISBN:
PB: 978-1-4729-2403-2
ePDF: 978-1-4729-2402-5

Library of Congress Cataloging-in-Publication Data
A catalog record for this book is available from the Library of Congress.

10 9 8 7 6 5 4 3 2 1

Printed and bound in India by Replika Press Pvt. Ltd.

This book is produced using paper that is made from wood grown in managed, sustainable forests. It is natural, renewable and recyclable. The logging and manufacturing processes conform to the environmental regulations of the country of origin.

To view more of our titles please visit www.bloomsbury.com

Acknowledgements
The authors would like to thank the following schools for their contribution to this book:
Battle Hill Primary School, North Tyneside
Birtley East Primary School, Gateshead
Bowburn Infant and Nursery School, Durham
Kells Lane Primary School, Gateshead
Newsham Primary School, Northumberland
Valley View Primary School, Jarrow

Contents

Introduction

This book aims to value and celebrate the special qualities of boys, their strengths, their character, their enthusiasm for learning and their zest for life.

Boys' underachievement is an issue across the entire developed world, and it is not going away! Only in Scandinavia do boys achieve at roughly the same rate as girls, and there they don't start school formally until they are seven. Prior to that, they are learning actively, outdoors and largely through play. It is a simple equation: for many boys in the UK and elsewhere, the demands made upon them to read and write before they are emotionally and physically ready to do so can give many an early taste of failure from which they may never fully recover.

It is not all boys that underachieve. It tends to be white working class boys from less financially stable backgrounds that are at the bottom of the heap. However, most boys will benefit from the practical guidance provided in this book. The advice and suggestions for improving practice will not be to the detriment of girls because anything that addresses the attitude, the behaviour and subsequently the performance of boys will have a positive effect for all. The themes and activities described are more often than not enjoyed by girls as well.

Positive, supportive work by pre-school providers and early years practitioners can be absolutely vital in breaking down some of the barriers to boys' achievement at the very beginning of their educational journey. Practical ideas for that supportive work forms the basis of this book. Sometimes very simple adjustments to the excellent practice of early years' staff can make a difference. For example, spending time focusing on helping boys develop fine motor skills will greatly reduce issues that may develop when they begin to write. The time boys spend learning through play outdoors will give them the opportunity to be themselves and learn in an environment where there is space and also ample natural resources to make noise, have freedom to move and explore and develop a real zest for learning.

Language skills

Language plays an important part in boys' development. Girls can use between ten and thirty times more language in their play than boys. We can help boys to become more confident in their use of language by ensuring that we create a wide variety of opportunities for talk in their early years. We also know that girls, by and large, tend to be more capable of talking about their emotions than boys. Even at a young age, boys can be encouraged to hide their emotions, often by their own peers ('boys don't cry') and sometimes by their fathers, too. In teaching, the development of emotional intelligence in youngsters is an essential element of what we need to nurture, and this should impact upon how we talk to boys and how we talk to girls. By ensuring that practitioners are aware of the importance of analysing how they talk to boys and girls respectively, they can make a significant difference to the way boys perceive themselves as learners. By giving boys the words with which to express their feelings, something at which girls tend to be far more adept, their emotional development will be significantly enhanced.

By engaging with parents, practitioners and teachers can help reduce parental anxieties and help boys to succeed. Showing parents how they can actively support their sons' language skills, help them develop a love of reading and encourage a positive attitude toward learning can have a major impact. Parents need to be aware how vital it is to help their sons' independence to ensure they become effective, self-sufficient learners. This book provides practical strategies, tools and workshop sessions that will help early years practitioners forge that vital partnership with parents.

Being aware of the negative stereotyping that often surrounds boys will help to ensure that, as practitioners, we don't fall foul of thinking 'boys will be boys!' and instead will encourage us to think 'boys will be ... brilliant!' Above all, perhaps, is the need for what is virtually an entirely female workforce to have the knowledge and the confidence to link into what's going on in a boy's head, a boy's world and a boy's universe. In early years education, as in all education, we need to value what it is that boys have to offer. With the commitment of informed and reflective early years practitioners, we can challenge negativity. We love working with boys, don't we? We love to see how enthusiastic and engaged they become when we work or play with them in ways that relate to their interests. We love their openness and honesty. What you see is what you get! We love the fact that they can be a little more challenging, which often means that they can also be that little bit more rewarding. We love their sense of fun and sense of humour, and we love the way that every day is a brand new day for them. Together we can strive to make every day an exciting and rewarding learning day for them.

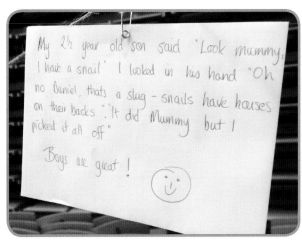

My 2½ year old son said "Look mummy, I have a snail" I looked in his hand "Oh no Daniel, thats a slug - snails have houses on their backs". It did Mummy but I picked it all off"

Boys are great! ☺

chapter 1

Gender differences

The way we see ourselves is shaped by the messages we receive from the significant people in our lives. Male and female babies are treated and handled differently from birth. Gendered behaviour is *learned* behaviour, and this begins from a very young age indeed.

Gendered behaviour in the early years ranges from children's own comments to each other about toys, about colours and about clothes, to the way they communicate and play together. But it is also true that we may find ourselves, as professionals, responding to boys and girls in ways that perpetuate these gender stereotypes too.

> *Educational consultants were observed describing three week old twins. They used the following words to describe the boy – 'big', 'a bouncer', 'sturdy'; the words used to describe the girl were 'precious', 'pretty', and 'gorgeous'.*

We want all the children in our care to feel that they are equally valued and loved. To this end, it is important that we examine our attitudes towards (and expectations of) both boys and girls. The 'Attitude checklist' on page 71 will provide a useful starting point for discussions, enabling adults in the setting to explore their behaviours and attitudes. What other differences in interactions—both supportive and unsupportive—have been noted?

- Use the 'Attitude checklist' on page 71 to help you reflect on the practice in your setting.

- What do you think might need to change?

It matters a great deal if boys interpret the way we speak to them as a sign that we prefer teaching girls, and that is what many boys feel. If you're still not convinced that we talk to boys and girls differently, how about this?

Picture the following scene in your mind: in the construction corner are a small group of boys and girls. There is the sudden noise of objects crashing to the floor. What phrases spring to the forefront of your mind? *'JORDAN! What are you doing!?' – 'Julie, are you alright?'* A wild exaggeration perhaps – or is there a hint of truth there?

> *A parent reported that at the end of her daughter's first week in nursery she could recite the full names of all the boys in nursery but only the first name of the girls!*
>
> *Another parent told a story of her daughter coming home on the first day in nursery. She said, 'there are two Neils in my nursery and one of them is called Neil Behave!'*

Negative labelling

Children are labelled by society from a very early age. This can be seen on clothing, for example, where young girls are labelled as 'little princesses' and young boys as 'little monsters'. Clearly this labelling serves no positive purpose, and rightful objections to girls being labelled in this way are frequently aired. With regards to boys, the labels appear to invite bad behaviour, as do the following sayings which are very common: 'well, he's a boy, what do you expect?,' or 'boys will be boys'. We may even hear these from parents and sometimes from our own mouths.

Therefore, as practitioners, we need to try to make parents and carers aware of the potential harm that negative labelling and negative stereotyping can have on boys. Boys can develop a negative image of themselves from wearing clothes with slogans that describe them as 'trouble', 'messy', etc. Representations in books and the media also encourage negative gender stereotypes, for example, many TV adverts portray males as either the swaggering macho male, or else the bumbling, useless husband in contast with the competent, organised wife.

ACTIVITY ★ ★ ★ ★ ★ ★ ★

As staff, collect and collate examples of gender stereotyping in the media, in toy catalogues, greeting cards and even your own reading area! How many picture books feature positive, caring male role models?

See list of suggested picture books that boys not only enjoy but which also show boys in non-stereotypical ways on page 63.

Discuss the above as starting points for addressing gender issues in your setting.

Maynard (2002) (see page 64) states that the choices parents make for their children (for example names, clothing, toys and hobbies) profoundly influence children's understanding of their gender role within their culture and society.

> *We know that to give boys and girls equal rights in the early years means to give them different and specific opportunities. It is not sufficient to say that everything… is open to all children, since at this age children choose gender specific activities.*
>
> Svaleryd in OECD, 2004

Why might boys underachieve in the early years classroom?

Boys are not less able than girls, but summative data shows that many boys do not achieve as well as girls in the early years. These early gender differences in achievement can establish a pattern that can continue throughout school. If we are to begin to close the gap between boys' and girls' achievement, we need to look at how we engage boys in the learning process.

We know, for example, that many boys find keeping still difficult. Boys tend to have an instinctive need for movement, activity and risk. Their natural exuberance and curiosity can sometimes be misinterpreted as inappropriate behaviour. We need to be sure that in our daily practice we become more aware of the needs of boys and more adept at valuing their strengths.

> *If teachers view boys' energetic, action-orientated activity as immature and disruptive and if teachers ask boys to conform to behaviour that they are not physically or emotionally ready for, then this can result in the seeds of boys' underachievement in education being sown in the early years.*
>
> Ouvry (2003:18).

There are many more barriers to boys' success in early years which will be explored in the following chapters. Perhaps one of the most crucial is the lack of independence that many boys exhibit when they begin their educational journey.

chapter 2

Developing independence

Generally, boys will happily allow the adults in their lives do everything for them. Parents and carers are often unaware that this can have an impact on their development. There is clear evidence to suggest that there is a strong correlation between children who are independent (who can put on their own coat, for example) prior to starting school, and their ability to develop as independent learners.

As practitioners, we understand that in order to be successful learners, boys need to become more independent. Often, however, there are some parents who, even with the best of intentions, feel their role is to do everything for their boys.

A practitioner reported that, 'mums often say he is too young to do this and that at home, but I know full well that he is perfectly capable of doing those things all day in school.'

Have you ever had experience of the following?

Parents who place a dummy in their child's mouth the moment they collect them from you.

Parents carrying their child in from the car, and then handing them into your arms. You just want to say 'but he has got legs!'.

Parents fussing about putting on their child's coat, and collecting their lunchbox, even though you know the child is perfectly capable of doing it themselves.

Discuss...

Do you notice any difference in a parent's behaviour and attitude when picking up a son or a daughter?

Discuss...

Do you notice the difference in behaviour and attitude when mum/female carer collects a boy, and when dad/male carer collects him?

Discuss...

Share your thoughts and feelings. What other examples have you observed?

As a first step to promoting boys' independence, you may want to produce information leaflets using some of the material presented in 'Activities to help with dressing' (page 72) and 'Q&A Card 1: Developing independence' (page 73). Photocopy these sheets and use them to support parents in developing their boys' independence.

You may consider using the following suggestions for developing boys' independence in the setting. Set challenges: boys respond positively to a challenge!

Use this to promote independence:

- I wonder if you can put your sweatshirt on by yourself before I turn around.

- I wonder if you can put the blocks away by yourself before the sand runs out.

Remember to give boys praise specific to what they have achieved independently. You could write a personal label 'Errol can now put on his own sweatshirt' that the child can wear proudly, announcing his achievement to his parents and the world. Upon seeing a child wearing these stickers, encourage any adult in the setting to reinforce their achievement by giving appropriate praise. This will communicate a clear message to parents that will encourage them to consolidate the praise and help raise their expectations of their child. Discuss what else you might do to promote the important issue of developing independence, for example, a display in the entrance to the setting.

You may wish to engage in a more powerful way through a series of meetings with parents as exemplified in the tried and tested format in Chapter 11.

Remember!
Have the same expectations of boys demonstrating independence as girls demonstrating independence.

Independent thinking and self-reflection

When boys are asked to review or reflect upon a learning situation, they often just want to race on towards the next thing. It can be quite a challenge to stop them mid flow, yet that is precisely what we must do. As they go through school, their ability to reflect on their learning becomes increasingly important if they are to be successful, independent learners.

Trying to learn without reviewing or reflecting is like trying to fill the bath without the plug in.

Mike Hughes

Consider using the following strategies:

TUMMMY TIME
All youngsters lie flat on their tummies facing inwards in a circle, heads propped up on hands, and discuss their learning. This is a good opportunity to get the children reflecting on what they have learned and which aspects of the learning they most enjoyed.

PHOTO RECORD
A common practice in early years that helps develop reflective skills is to take photographs of the children playing and learning. Invite them to talk to their parents and to practitioners about what is going on in the photograph. You can extend this by inviting children to record their description into a talking tin or talking postcard and display it next to the photograph so that anyone can share what the child has recorded and have a conversation with them about it. Discuss other methods you use to encourage reflection and what other strategies you might introduce.

Emotional development

Many boys have difficulty naming and expressing their own feelings. Sometimes they just know they don't feel quite right. Some boys don't have the words to identify the feeling of being sad, cross, scared or worried. They may say they are hungry when actually they are tired! It is vitally important that we help boys to understand and express their emotions. Sometimes boys can find it difficult to read non-verbal cues and may respond inappropriately.

Until they can understand and express their own feelings, boys will have difficulty empathising and building relationships with others.

> *Girls become more adept at reading both verbal and non-verbal emotional signals, at expressing and communicating their feelings and boys become adept at minimising emotions having to do with vulnerability, guilt, fear and hurt.*
>
> **Brody and Hall, 1993**

Often male peers will encourage boys not to cry, which will further pressurise them into keeping their feelings hidden. This situation may also be encouraged if older males in the home frequently tell their boy to 'man up'. To try and avoid this, the adults close to the child need to honour their tender feelings.

Discuss...

Discuss with your colleagues any differences you have noticed between boys and girls when it comes to expressing or dealing with emotions. What do you do that works? What else could you try?

A teacher is told by a girl in the reception class that one of the boys has brought a lighter into school. When the teacher demands to see the lighter, the boy hands it over and immediately he bursts into tears:

'I am going to be in so much trouble with my dad.'

'I am not surprised,' said the teacher, 'bringing a lighter into school ...

'Not that, for crying, I mean.'

Discuss...

Have you ever found yourself reacting in a completely different way to a boy who is crying because he is upset compared to a boy who has kicked over a chair because he is upset?

Discuss...

Do you explicitly teach and model 'emotion words'?

Discuss...

Do you regularly ask boys how they are feeling?

As a simple first step in promoting boys' emotional well-being, you could share the information sheet, 'Q&A Card 2: Supporting emotional development' (page 74) with parents and carers. Make photocopies and use them to support parents in developing boys' emotional well-being. Discuss and share other ways in which you can help to raise parents' awareness of the issues around boys and emotional development in the home and in your setting.

Developing emotional well-being in your setting

Peer massage

Many boys experience minimal positive touch in their home lives. Some may experience none at all. Peer massage can help significantly when it comes to creating the right emotional environment for learning after an energetic or rough lunchtime. It also helps to calm down 'macho' or 'laddish' behaviour. Studies show that five to ten minutes of massage per day leads to a rise in concentration and alertness. It makes the environment a calmer place, with a reduction in aggressive behaviour and an increase in self-esteem and respect. As the 'Massage in Schools Programme' (**www.massageinschools.com**) also asserts: 'The effects of massage are immediate … yet they can last a lifetime.' Parents can be encouraged to build peer massage into their child's bedtime routine.

Peer massage is used widely across the UK and can have huge benefits to children's emotional health and well-being. It also helps to develop listening and attention and fine motor skills. It is used in settings, in schools and across whole Local Authorities. In Rochdale, for example, peer massage has been introduced into every primary school as part of their personal, social and emotional development programme.

'I am the decisive element in the classroom.

It is my personal approach that creates the climate.

It is my daily mood that makes the weather.

As a teacher I possess tremendous power to make a child's life miserable or joyous. I can be a tool of torture or an instrument of inspiration. I can humiliate or humour, hurt or heal. It is my response that decides whether a crisis will be escalated or de-escalated, a child humanised or dehumanised.'

Ginott, 1972

Critical to the emotional well-being of all of our children is their sense of self-worth which to quite a degree depends upon the approval or disapproval of those around them from their early years. The power and the responsibility this brings cannot be overstated. The way in which we talk to boys (and girls too, of course) will clearly define their sense of self-worth and subsequently have a huge impact on their emotional development.

Remember!
Emotional intelligence starts with us!

Physical development

There is clear evidence that many boys in the early years are significantly behind in the development of their fine and gross motor skills. For boys who have less well-developed motor skills, sitting with their legs crossed can create a barrier to their learning. They will concentrate on keeping still and balancing on three points of their body, rather than focussing on what they are being taught. Similarly, expecting boys to write before they are physically able to do so can often give them an early taste of failure, from which many of them may never fully recover. In the early years it is vital that we explicitly support boys with the development of gross and fine motor skills. To do this we must start big – preferably outdoors!

> *Physical development underpins all other areas of learning. The Millennium Cohort Study of nearly 15,000 children stated that babies who were slow to develop their motor skills at nine months were significantly more likely to be identified as behind in their cognitive development and also likely to be less well behaved at age five.*

> *A parent reported that at the end of her boy's first day in school he said, 'I don't like school mummy. It hurts.' It transpired that the child had been asked to write the letter 'a' over and over again.*
>
> *A teacher observed that a boy began crying every time he was asked to write. She discussed this with his mum, who offered the information that she was helping by making him do handwriting exercises every night!*
>
> *Do you ever hear boys complain that their hand hurts when holding a pencil?*
>
> *Share your thoughts and feelings, what other examples have you observed.*

You must make it your priority to ensure that parents don't become overly anxious about what their boys need to be able to do before starting school. The worksheet 'Taking the pressure off' (page 75) provides reassurance to parents that just because their son can't read or write this does not mean he isn't 'school ready.' Very often we find that a parent's anxiety is often reflected in their boys. 'Writing is more than holding a pencil and making marks' (page 76) supplies parents (and practitioners) with practical ideas to help them help their boy develop fine motor skills.

Make photocopies of these useful sheets and use them to support parents developing boys' gross and fine motor skills.

Developing fine and gross motor skills in your setting

Materials and resources to use in the **outdoor** area:

- Builder trays: filled with cornflour gloop, shaving foam, mud

- Mud kitchen, with a range of large and small utensils

- Beanbags, balls of various sizes for throwing and catching

- Hoops, buckets and baskets

- Scooters, balance bikes, two-wheeled bikes and trikes

- Wobble boards

- Chalk boards and whiteboards

- Large sheets of paper for co-operative drawing/ writing activities

- Sheets of Perspex for painting on

- Water pistol, squeeze bottles, buckets of water with large brushes, bottles of water with thin brushes

- Individual writing packs (bum bags)

- Material with a selection of pegs, karabiners, clips for joining and attaching

- Cover the underside of an old table with paper for drawing on

- Natural resources: twigs, shells small logs etc.

- Large wooden blocks, crates, drain pipes

- Logs for walking along, balancing on and jumping off

- A central bank of writing materials and resources

Remember!
Clay is a particularly boy-friendly material for helping develop fine motor skills.

Materials and resources that could be freely available in a fine motor skills area **inside:**

MATERIALS FOR DEVELOPING SCRUNCHING AND PULLING MOVEMENTS

- Lycra squares
- Squashy balls
- Stretchy bands
- Sponges
- Elastic bands

MATERIALS FOR DEVELOPING PAINTING AND WRITING MOVEMENTS

Trays with:

- Rice
- Couscous
- Shaving foam
- Finger paint

MATERIALS FOR DEVELOPING PINCER MOVEMENTS

- Tweezers
- Buttons for posting into jars, boxes etc.
- Wind-up toys
- Pipe cleaners
- Sprung clothes pegs
- Kitchen tongs

ADDITIONAL ACTIVITIES TO DEVELOP FINE MOTOR CONTROL

- Paint with cotton buds
- Stick uncooked spaghetti into a ball of dough. Thread cut up setions of straws onto the spaghetti
- Use melon scoops to scoop up coloured aquarium gravel into ice cube trays
- Add soap flakes to water and whisk until thick and frothy. After whisking, children can model with the thick mixture
- Hide interesting objects in a ball of dough, e.g. coloured glass beads, small shells
- Use finger and thumb to put coloured aquarium gravel into a Tic Tac™ box or similar small plastic container

MATERIALS FOR DEVELOPING THREADING MOVEMENTS

- Cardboard tubes cut into pieces
- Bobbins
- Large beads
- Buttons
- Small beads
- Using doweling
- Using plastic washing line
- Paper clips

Use all areas of the setting when planning activities to support boys' development of fine motor skills – and never mind just in early years! Have that box of lumps of play dough, sticky tack, stress balls and pipe cleaners on their table all through primary school. Apart from anything else, how often have you heard yourself say, 'look, stop fiddling with that. Put it down and listen to me!'?

Discuss the kinds of methods/activities you have found useful in your setting/school and what other activities you may want to introduce. Also, discuss what other kinds of activities you might suggest to parents to try at home.

chapter 5

Developing language and communication

Language and communication skills are vital to the development of learning as well as to a child's social and emotional well-being. They support the development of reading and writing. It is generally understood that girls tend to develop language skills at a faster rate than boys and use more language in their play. This delay in boys' language development can clearly be a barrier to learning. A systematic approach to the teaching of language and communication skills is necessary if boys are going to make progress.

> One practitioner was amazed when the headteacher asked a boy (in his second term of nursery) who was playing in the sand tray, to pass him a rake. The boy picked up a spade and handed it over. A girl quickly stepped in and proudly handed a rake to the headteacher, saying, 'no, this is a rake!' Nobody had taught the boy the name of the objects in the sand area.

> One reception class teacher had great success in helping a boy who had difficulty in remembering the beginning, middle and end of a story. The teacher adopted a systematic 'Talk for Writing' approach, which involved telling the story with actions and rehearsing the story over and over. Within a week the child was able to re-tell a simple story in the correct sequence.

Discuss...
It is known that boys need around ten seconds of thinking time before they can answer a question, whereas girls need considerably less time. Do staff give boys enough thinking time to answer before asking another question?

Discuss...
Do all staff expand language by scaffolding and adding words? (E.g. Child: 'I drew a butterfly.' Adult: 'Yes, you drew a red butterfly. It's beautiful.')

Discuss...
Do you notice differences between the language and communication skills used by some boys and girls?

Discuss...
Do speaking and listening develop 'accidentally' at your school or do you have a clear programme for oral communication?

Creating spaces

Elizabeth Jarman's approach to communication (see *The Communication Friendly Spaces Approach*) encourages the creation of special places for boys to talk.

SECRET SPACES E.g. long grass with a pathway cut into it and small open spaces.

PLACES TO BUILD These provide a rich language-learning environment that specifically engages boys in estimating, planning and reflecting.

PLACES THAT ARE COSY Areas for children to enjoy books, with related props and figures.

A PLACE FOR GROUP NEGOTIATION E.g. in an area where there might be a number of flat packed boxes and other open-ended materials.

A SPACE TO RETREAT AND REFLECT E.g. dens.

Discuss...
Within your setting, do you provide a range of communication-friendly spaces which encourage boys to communicate with one another?

Language at home

Of course most early language is developed in the home. It may be useful to explore parents' experience of their child(ren)'s early language skills. As a simple first step in promoting boys' communication and language skills, you could share the 'Q&A Cards 3 and 4: Supporting early literacy development' (pages 77 and 78) with parents and carers by photocopying them and using them to support parents in developing boys' early literacy skills.

Teaching attention and listening skills

Turn-taking games work really well for boys who love the challenge of listening intently for the signal indicating that it is their turn.

- Ready steady go/stop games. These can be played with any resource, e.g. putting compare bears into a container.

- Songs where they have to listen for the signal word or phrase, e.g. 'sleeping bunnies – wake up!'

- Musical games, e.g. 'musical bumps'.

- Follow the leader games, e.g. 'Simon says…'.

Developing speaking and understanding skills

- Use daily routines and activities to introduce vocabulary and concepts.

- Give children time to begin a 'conversation'.

- When joining in with children's play, verbally describe what you are doing and what the child is doing , i.e. give a running commentary.

- Model by repeating the child's sentence in a more 'mature' form:
  Child: 'Him's eat biscuit.'
  Adult: 'Yes, he is eating a biscuit.'

- Communicate choices simply. For example, instead of asking 'where do you want to play?', you may need to ask a child with limited understanding to choose between two options. You could use photographs of the choices to help develop their understanding.

- Ensure that all children – particularly boys – get at least one small group (one adult to two children) 'book experience' a week. Use these sessions to teach vocabulary and understanding.

Many children have limited opportunities to talk at home. Fewer than half the homes in the UK have got tables around which families sit and eat and talk, not to mention the omnipresence of computers, tablets, phones and television screens in homes with their accompanying background noise and distractions.

A particular influence on young children's acquisition of language is the effect of shared book reading with adults. Findings show that early expressive language development was facilitated by joint reading strategies that engaged, supported and promoted children's active participation in the book reading opportunities.

The longer a child stayed engaged in the book reading episode, and the more an adult encouraged the child's active participation by expanding on what a child says, or by asking open-ended questions, the greater the effect the reading experience had on the child's language development.

Trivette CM, Dunst CJ, Gorman E. *Effects of parent-mediated joint book reading on the early language development of toddlers and pre-schoolers*. Centre for Early Literacy Learning (CELL) Reviews 2010; 3(2):1-15.

Storytelling area

Consider setting up a storytelling area. This will help develop the love of story that is so important, and will give boys an additional incentive to use the language of stories in their play.

Make it special by providing some of the following:

- Story teller's chair or an adult-sized sofa

- Storyteller's hat

- Magic carpet

- Story music

- Fairy lights

- Props, story books, story maps for children to use when they re-tell stories

Boys need to rehearse their ideas orally. If they can't tell a story they will struggle to write one.

Remember!
Many children have limited book experiences before school. Developing a love of stories therefore is vital in the early years, particularly for boys, who may be more naturally drawn to other activities.

Discuss...
Discuss the things that you have done to excite and engage boys in reading. What else could you do?

chapter 6

Developing an outdoor learning environment with added boy appeal

Outdoor learning has a positive impact on children's well-being and development. Its particular value, as far as boys are concerned, is that it gives them the freedom to explore, to use their senses and to be physically active and imaginative. Outdoor learning is enhanced by an environment that is richly resourced with exciting play materials and open-ended flexible resources. Boys enjoy being able to adapt and use resources in different ways and will use them to foster their interests. For example, a pine cone can be a tree in small world play or it could hold special magical powers in imaginative play.

The outdoor environment is more effective when adults focus on what can be learnt from the resources available rather than focussing on what additional resources and equipment they need. If all children – but particularly boys – are to make the most of the open-ended resources and materials available to them, they should have open access to the indoor and outdoor learning environment and be able to move freely between the two environments.

When planning or developing the outdoor environment, remember that water enriches children's play and learning. A variety of hard (tarmac, gravel) and soft (grass, mud) surfaces can spark boys' imaginations. For example, the mud can become the swamp where the monster lives.

Remember:

- The outdoor learning environment should not simply replicate the provision from indoor areas.

- Indoors and outdoors need to be viewed as one combined and integrated environment.

- All the resources and materials need not be accessible to children all of the time.

- Be selective and rotate the range of resources available. Use resources flexibly.

- The outdoor learning environment should provide for learning opportunities that are 'bigger, messier and noisier!'

- Create a storage and retrieval system so that children can access and return resources independently.

- Create a central resource for writing, mathematical and investigational equipment and materials.

- Allow boys in their play to transport resources from one area of the learning environment to any other areas.

Do you give the indoor and outdoor learning environment equal value?

Discuss...

What works well indoors and what works well outdoors?

If there is an imbalance, what do you need to do to develop a better balance?

Outdoor areas

This is not an exhaustive list but it gives ideas for areas and resources that are likely to engage and motivate boys.

Remember that equipment needs to be bigger in some outdoor areas in order to engage boys. For example, provide large metal colanders, bowls and buckets in the outdoor sand area rather than replicating the plastic indoor sand equipment.

Mud/mixing area

- Sand, compost, pebbles, rocks

- Water in a container or access to a tap

- Sticks for stirring and mixing

- Petals, flower heads, herbs, fragrant plants and leaves

- A range of baking tins, trays, jelly or cake moulds and pans

- Small plastic bottles with lids

- Large and small bowls, colanders, jugs, large and small bowls

- Funnels, measuring jugs, basters and pipettes

- Mixing utensils including a range of ladles, spoons, whisks, graters and mashers

- Measuring spoons, assorted sizes of pastry cutters, muffin and cake tins

- Laminated recipes, pictures of food and meals, white boards

- Brushes, lollipop sticks, twigs, ribbons, tape

- Candles, numbers

- Seed trays, baking trays and different sized plant pots

- Pestle and mortar

- Wire cooling rack, chopping board

- Beads, jewels, shells, leaves, feathers and stamps for decorating

- Magnifying glasses.

Water/sand/gravel area

- Outdoor tap

- Plastic and foil trays

- A wide range of brushes (from fine painting to wallpaper) and paint rollers

- Water containers with different diameters

- Buckets and sponges

- Washing-up bowls, washing line and a variety of pegs

- Bubbles, bubble wands, food colourings

- Soap flakes, washing up liquid, a variety of whisks

- Funnels, bowls, bottles, water pumps, turkey basters, jugs, watering cans

- Large moulds, empty plastic containers

- Cardboard boxes

- Builders' tray

- Natural materials: pebbles, stones, shells, feathers, leaves, flowers, gravel, sticks, twigs, driftwood, lollipop sticks, corks

- Things that float: ping pong balls, boats, trays

- Small world animals, dinosaurs, cars and people

- Trucks and diggers

- Water pistols or squeezy bottles

- Cups and teapot for domestic play

- Large metal scoops, bowls, pans, colanders

- A plank to fit across the water container or sand pit.

Open-ended role play area

- A prop box compiled around a particular theme or a story

- A frame or clothes-horse, or canes

- Washing line and pegs

- Cardboard boxes in various shapes and sizes

- The sides of cardboard boxes

- Camouflage net

- Crates

- Material, a variety of pegs, tape, hair scrunchies and cable ties

- Silver rescue blankets

- Plastic sheets

- Pop up tent

- Large blocks

- Large tubes

- Microphone

- Hats

- Bags

- String

- Back pack, lunch box

- Carpet squares.

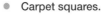

Construction area

- Commercial kits (that require space)

- Large wooden blocks

- Cardboard boxes

- Natural blocks from sawn branches

- Guttering, tubes

- Fabric, blankets, rugs, ground sheets, pegs, string and tape

- Natural materials

- Hard hats

- Buckets

- Spirit level, tape measure

- Chalk

- A selection of large vehicles

- Carpet squares

- Remote controlled cars/Beebots™

- Clipboards, long sheets of paper for drawing plans

- Mobile phone

- Construction site signs

- Site warning tape

- Wheel barrow

- Cement mixer

- Cones

- Photographs of buildings

- Toy or ride-on vehicles.

Quiet/book area

- A frame and material to make an enclosure or a corner space

- Seating

- A hammock

- Large umbrella or parasol

- Carpet squares, blankets, rugs

- Wind chimes, wind socks, CDs hanging

- Sensory toys

- Herbs to smell and touch

- Natural materials

- Pop-up tent or gazebo

- Puppets

- Books

- Portable CD player and CD with quiet, relaxing music.

Gross/fine motor area

- Ribbon sticks

- Pompoms

- Lengths of lycra and material

- Scarves, large feathers

- Balls, hoops, beanbags

- Chopsticks

- Plastic spray bottles

- Brushes, buckets

- Paint rollers and trays

- Large chalk board

- Aqua mat or builder's tray

- Dust pan and brushes

- A-frames

- Plastic crates/guttering/planks of wood/blocks/ ground sheets

- String/rope/pegs

- Tunnels

- Cardboard boxes

- Masking tape

- Tree trunk sections.

Music area

- Hanging musical chimes, musical instruments, rainmakers

- Metal lids, spoons

- Wooden, plastic, metal beaters

- Natural material for shaking and dropping into plastic metal containers

- Musical mat

- Tubes to use as megaphones

- Microphone

- Portable CD player and CDs

- Stage area, mats, rugs, blankets.

Develop prop boxes around boys' interests

Car wash

CONTENTS OF PROP BOX

- Buckets and sponges

- Cloths

- Brushes (various)

- 'Car wash', 'Entry', 'Exit' signs

- Open/closed notices

- Cones, chalk for car parking lines, arrows etc.

- Price list

- Car shampoos etc. (clean empty bottles)

- Old garden hose

- Clock, till and money, computer keyboard, appointments book, pens and pencils

- Watering cans

- Caps, boots, overalls for car washers

- Lost property box label

- Magazines and newspapers

- Larger equipment trikes or cars etc. for washing.

SUGGESTED ACTIVITIES

★ Make a car wash token machine from a box; talk about the difference between tokens and real money

★ Explore the difference soap or detergent makes to cleaning things

★ Observe and talk about what happens when things get wet, and how and why things dry

★ Observe puddles drying

★ Draw car tracks and directions on the ground

★ Blow bubbles and talk about the colours you can see in them

★ Number parking bays

★ Make a list of car licence plates.

Pizza delivery

CONTENTS OF PROP BOX

- Pizza boxes (small ones are easier to handle)

- Satchel or carrying bag

- Bike helmet for deliveries

- Menus, including list of toppings (pictorial)

- Money and bag

- Notebook for delivery addresses

- Street map

- Mobile phones

- Telephone

- Telephone directory

- Dough recipes and dough or fake pizzas from salt dough or circles of cardboard with painted toppings

- Chef's apron, checked trousers, hat

- Pizza wheels

- Paper napkins

- Cutters and rollers

- Magazines and newspapers

- Posters

LARGER EQUIPMENT

- Trike or bike for deliveries

- Large cardboard box with 'door' cut out to act as an oven

- Table to act as a counter

- Chairs to wait on.

SUGGESTED ACTIVITIES

★ As a group or class, have a pizza delivered to your setting

★ Read the menu, choose your pizza and order your pizza by phone – discuss the need to give the correct address

★ Arrange for the delivery person to talk to the children as they eat the pizza

★ Make a pizza shop from boxes etc.

★ Write a pizza menu

★ Complete order forms

★ Act out roles: delivery man, customer, chef

★ Read the story 'The Royal Palace'.

Building site

CONTENTS OF PROP BOX

- Red and white tape
- Cones
- Work signs
- Hard hats
- Fluorescent jackets
- Hand tools
- Sanding blocks
- Buckets
- Spirit levels
- Trowels, spades
- Overalls
- Tape measure
- Metre rule
- Sorting boxes with nails/screws
- Sand

LARGER EQUIPMENT

- Wooden blocks, cardboard boxes, crates
- Large plastic or house bricks
- Pop up tent
- Plastic pipe.

SUGGESTED ACTIVITIES

- ★ Draw a plan of the building
- ★ Tape off part of the area – discuss safety
- ★ Take photographs of the finished building
- ★ Write signs, e.g. 'men at work!'
- ★ Make rubbings of textured surfaces within the setting
- ★ Mix cement and observe the change.

chapter 7

Developing an indoor learning environment with added boy appeal

In order to create a rich, enabling indoor learning environment it is important that all children – but particularly boys – have access to stimulating resources which are accessible and open-ended and which are relevant to their interests.

Indoor spaces should be used flexibly and should change in response to boys' interests and fascinations. Boys tend to only use resources that they can 'see.' They don't always like having to 'look' for resources in cupboards or drawers. To facilitate boys accessing resources, ensure that the resources are visually orderly. It is important that you don't constantly change resources as boys need time to explore ideas and interests at length and in depth. Giving boys a five-minute warning (visual as well as audible) before tidy-up time will prevent them being too frustrated: 'I don't like it when I just start doing something, then I have to tidy up and I haven't finished.' Consider providing a holding bay for unfinished models (see the photograph below).

Boys flourish in a safe but challenging indoor learning environment.

Indoor resources

The following lists of resources are not exhaustive but they can be used as useful checklists to ensure that there are resources that will engage and motivate boys within the learning environment.

Role play

In addition to or instead of a home corner you may want to develop a role play that builds on boys' interests (but would still appeal to girls). Consider the following ideas:

- Space station

- Bat cave

- Spiderman's den

- Police station.

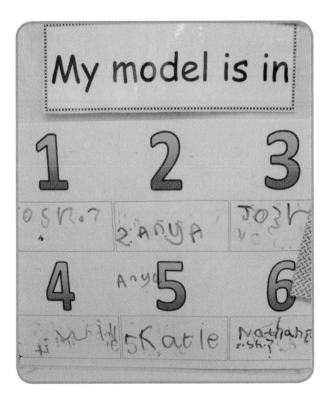

Home area

- Home furniture – cooker, oven, fridge, microwave, sink, washer, table and chairs, bed, cot, settee, etc.

- Real life equipment e.g. TV, laptop, iPad, telephone, radio, camera, calculator

- Dressing-up clothes and accessories (some to develop awareness of other cultures). These can be open-ended materials e.g. bags, hats etc.

- Appropriate writing materials

- Whiteboard/message board

- Meaningful contexts for writing and reading, shopping lists, birthday cards, recipes, take-away menus and telephone directories

- Books, comics, newspapers, car magazines, recipe books, signs and labels

- Magazine rack

- Resources to support mathematical development – boxes, bottles, packets of varying sizes, sets of coloured crockery cutlery, priced items and coins

- Cups, saucers, etc. (you could even use china so that children can be taught to handle with care!)

- Salt dough food, tins, boxes, dried pasta, real fruit

- Pots, kettles, toaster, pans – to include wok set, stainless steel and baking trays

- Tea towel, washing-up liquid, clothes to be used as laundry, spray bottle containing water

- Dolls to reflect different genders and cultures

- Baby equipment and toys

- Telescope/binoculars

- Screws, nuts and bolts to sort and organise

- Screw drivers and spanners

- Tool kits

- Plastic interlocking plumbing pipes

- Enhancements linked to popular culture, theme, topic or event, or children's interests

- Animals – pet basket and pet

- Birthday props - balloons, badges etc.

- Mother's day and father's days – vase of flowers and card.

Writing area

- Open shelving to store resources

- Flat table

- A selection of different types of paper and card in a variety of sizes

- Selection of writing implements, washable fibre tip pens, selection of pencils, chalks, coloured pencils, crayons of different thicknesses. Provide a variety of pen grips and differently weighted pencils etc.

- Grapheme cards, name cards, examples of environmental print (Nursery) – begin with key words, then progress to story starters (Reception). Link to topic or theme as appropriate

- Stamps, ink pads, Magna Doodle, whiteboards and a variety of wipe-clean pens (these resources are popular with boys as they represent risk-free writing)

- Universal scissors (designed for both left- and right-handed users)

- Joining materials – treasury tags, split pins, paper clips, glue, sticky tack, sticky tape, masking tape

- Eraser, pencil sharpener, hole punch, ruler

- Books and artefacts (related topic or theme)

- Headed stationery, lined/squared paper, forms, post its/note pads

- Envelopes, stamps

- Ready-made books, zig-zag, stapled, unstapled

- Character wrapping paper for making cards and invitations

- Greeting cards

- Logs for creating wax rubbings

- Shells, pebbles, leaves etc. to draw around

- Writing frames linked to topic or theme

- 'Writing glasses' (sunglasses with the lens removed)

- 'Writing hats' (with special powers!) and 'writing bracelets' (reflective bands that click around the wrist of their writing hand)

- A display area where children can display their own writing.

Movement area

- Bubble wrap

- Keys and locks

- Tweezers

- Small containers

- Wind-up toys

- Pipe cleaners

- Gloop

- Shaving foam

- Nuts and bolts

- Plungers

- Stress balls

- Lycra

- Material for threading.

Book area

- Comfortable seating – settees (full size if possible), floor cushions (bean bags may not be a good idea), and floor should be carpeted

- A range of appropriate, good quality books, in good condition – include story, picture, dual language and non-fiction books

- Front-facing bookcase from which books can be easily accessed. (No more than ten fiction books)

- A character, a cuddly toy or a doll for children to read to/with

- Puppets matched to the stories, displayed together. (No more than three at any one time)

- A story sack linked to theme or topic, containing a character doll, small world resources or puppet related to the story

- Reading scheme books e.g. *Project X*

- Comics, magazines and catalogues

- Books written by the children

- Pictures/models/photographs/posters relating to stories and boys' interests

- Display of males reading (celebrities, older boys, male role models from the school community)

- Story maps

- CD player, CDs and book sets or storyphones®

- Easi speak® microphones (for boys to record stories)

- Plants/drapes/structures to make the area stimulating/aesthetically pleasing.

Dough/malleable materials area

- Basic dough with additions, e.g. coloured, plain, textured with sawdust, lentils etc., with flavouring and different smells

- Clay and clay tools

- Variety of doughs with different textures and elasticities

- Flour/water to change texture

- Cutters, pattern makers, rollers, knives, scissors

- Pasta, buttons, corks, nuts, bolts and washers

- Rolling pins

- Potato masher, garlic press, dough extruders

- Candles (cut up plastic straws), cake tins, cake cases

- Shelf or pretend oven to 'cook' cakes etc.

Scrap materials/modelling area

- A large flat table

- Enough shelving to store different materials in separate containers

- Character wrapping paper

- Scissors, pencils, felt pens, ruler, glue pots, glue spreaders

- Joining materials e.g. PVA, glue stick, paper clips and paper fasteners of different sizes, sticky tape, masking tape, string, ribbon, wool, elastic bands, stapler, hole punch

- Card in a variety of thicknesses and sizes

- Selection of paper

- Boxes, tubes and paper bags in a variety of sizes

- A variety of pastas, pulses and beans

- Fabric

- Polystyrene trays

- Tissue paper, crepe paper, cellophane

- Selection of natural materials (leaves, fir cones, twigs etc.).

Creative area

- Easels and table for painting

- Shelf unit for storage of materials

- Aprons

- Brushes in a range of sizes

- Paper in a range of sizes, weights and colours

- Powder paint, to include a 'hot' set and 'cold' set of colours, plus black and white

- Mixing pallets

- Paint pots

- Water colour blocks/boxes

- Ready mixed paint in containers that children can access independently

- A child-friendly drying rack

- A variety of paint additions including glue, paste, washing up liquid, sawdust, sand, lentils

- Felt pens, crayons, pencils and a range of mark-making tools – scourers, feathers, spatulas, foam rollers, etc.

- Aqua mat (risk free writing that dries up and disappears).

Maths investigation area

It is not essential that this area has a table, many boys work better on the floor as there is more space for them to count (lining up objects etc.)

- Peg boards

- Dominoes

- Natural materials e.g. pebbles, shells and conkers

- Sorting trays, boxes, shiny gift bags, baskets

- Plastic, wooden and magnetic numerals, number fans

- Rulers and tape measures

- Balance scales added when appropriate

- Money

- Laces and threading equipment

- Calculators

- Games and number puzzles as appropriate

- Interactive number line

- Number rhymes and matching resources

- Pencils

- Whiteboards and pens

- Squared paper.

Block area, construction area and small world area

- A variety of large and small construction sets

- Large wooden blocks, large plastic bricks, small wooden bricks

- Hard hats

- Construction equipment that provides opportunities to develop different manipulative skills (e.g. twist, snap, screw): Polydron, Clixi, Lego, Duplo, Meccano, Bau play, Brio Mec, Quadro

- Train set

- Post-its

- Sticky tack, masking tape, scissors

- Straws

- Lolly sticks

- Labels

- Writing implements, clip boards, whiteboards

- Paper and card

- Play characters from popular culture, play people

- Doll's furniture

- Models, such as vehicles, farm and wild animals, insects, dinosaurs, dragons, reptiles

- Selection of natural materials (leaves, fir cones, twigs etc.)

- Posters, information books on topics such as bridges, buildings and farms, jungles

- Tool kit

- Maps and local A-Z.

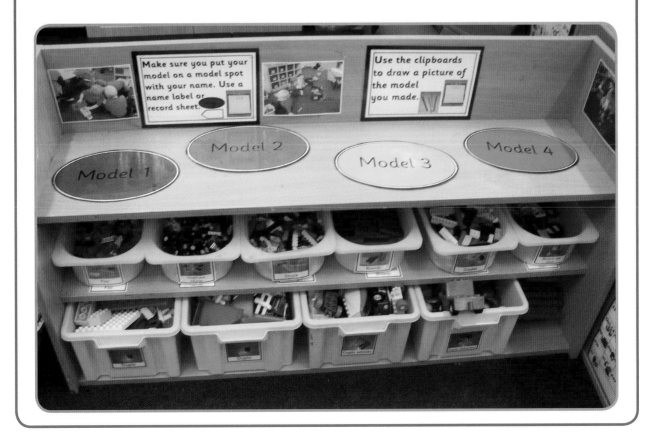

Science investigation area

- Light box or overhead projector

- Colour paddles and coloured cellophane

- Magnifying glasses

- Freestanding magnifiers

- Shells, conkers fir cones, leaves, twigs, flowers, stones, and fossils

- Magnets

- Mirrors

- Collection of mechanical items e.g. clocks, watches

- Snails, worms and caterpillars, as appropriate!

- Books and simple information cards linked to topic or theme

- Collections of materials including: textiles, taste, smell, seasons, seashore, countryside, food, rubbings, wood, stone, animal, fossils, etc.

- Paper, pencils, books

- Materials to enable children to grow plants e.g. seeds, compost, cuttings, pots, containers, watering cans, small tools

- Seasonal twigs, blossom, cut flowers

- Appropriate animals and insects e.g. fish, guinea pigs, rabbits, worms, ants, snails, caterpillars, stick insects etc.

- Torches, binoculars

- Easi scope microscope.

Sand area

- Materials to develop narratives and promote imaginative play

- Toy models such as dinosaurs, sea creatures, animals, people etc.

- Laminated photographs of children in the class with a small sticky tack base

- Selection of natural materials, e.g. leaves, fir cones, twigs, shells, stones rocks, corks, feathers, driftwood

- Whiteboards, pens

- Plastic tubing, drain pipe

- Jugs, buckets, funnels, spoons and bowls, graduated in size

- Sieves, wheels spades, trowels, moulds and scoops

- Containers of different sizes and shapes

- Lollipop sticks, art straws

- Paper, pencils

- Scissors to make flags, labels, notices

- Information books

- Dustpan and brush

- 'Tuff spots' can be used for sand and water, indoors and out

- Small individual trays can be used for sand, gloop, jelly, pasta, rice, oats, compost. One use is to trace letter shapes to help develop fine motor skills and help prepare for writing.

Water area

- Clean water, changed daily

- Child-sized mop and bucket

- Protective clothing

- A range of standard and non-standard containers of varying sizes (with and without holes)

- Funnels, tubing, pumps, sieves, wheels, buckets, sponges

- Off-cuts of waste pipes and guttering

- Variety of liquid containers e.g. soap dispenser, washing-up liquid bottles

- Fish, sea creatures, deep sea monsters, boats, play people, pirates

- Natural materials eg driftwood, pebbles, shells

- Paper, pencils, scissors to make flags, labels, notices

- Boxes/trays/baskets to store resources, labelled with name and picture

- Add bubbles, colouring, ice, soap flakes

- Soap, flannels, sponges, etc. for washing toy cars and character models or dolls

- Soap flakes for washing dolls and character clothes, with pegs and washing line to hang them out to dry.

Open-ended role play area

- Cardboard boxes, masking tape, string, wool

- Fabric

- Variety of pegs

- Pens, pencils and paper in a variety of sizes (from small labels to rolls of paper)

- Scissors, toolkit, joining materials

- Character wallpaper

- Bags, hats, scarves

- Disguise kits, masks, magic wands

- Encourage children to find other matrerials they may need from other areas of the classroom.

Music area

- Simple, un-tuned instruments, e.g. cymbals, bells, maracas, claves, guiro, shakers, drums, tambourines, tambours, triangles

- Tuned instruments e.g. xylophones, chime bars

- Easi-speak® microphone

- CDs of songs, rhymes and music, including those from other cultures

- Books of nursery rhymes, poems

- Materials to provide a variety of sounds: home-made shakers, squeaky toys, sandpaper blocks

- Listening games

- 'Props' or puppets to be used with songs and rhymes e.g. speckled frogs, ducks.

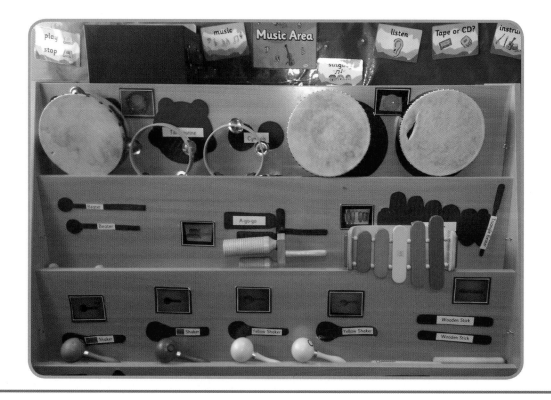

Using popular culture within the indoor and outdoor learning environment to engage, excite and motivate boys

On a simpler level, popular culture can be incorporated into your small world area, construction area, writing area and creative area by using:

- Party tablecloths, showing large-scale characters and landscapes that can be pinned to the wall. Children can then add their own laminated speech bubbles or add post-it notes

- Character wrapping paper cut to A4 size (useful in the creative area or in the writing area to encourage them to make cards etc.)

- Pens, pencils, notepaper and stickers depicting popular culture

- Positioning small superhero or film character figures in the small world area – sitting them on the table in the writing area will encourage boys to go there

- Mud, stones, string and sticks (to encourage boys to make homes for the superheroes)

- Pop up tents for making role play dens

- Party cups, saucers, novelties in the home corner (use character related invitations for them to invite their 'guests').

Use the site **www.imdb.com** to view and use photos from any film and to watch trailers.

chapter 8

The role of staff in supporting boys' learning

To ensure that both the indoor and outdoor environments maximise boys' learning potential, staff should complete an 'Observation survey' at least once every half term (see page 79). This should ideally comprise a series of around four ten-minute sample observations, carried out throughout different points in the day.

For example, the focus of one of your sample observations may be to evaluate whether:

- all areas/resources are accessed by both girls and boys equally;

- boys are actively or passively involved and engaging with the provision;

- the provision promotes the boys', as well as the girls', language development.

Following your observation survey, complete the *'What are you going to do next?'* box on the sheet (page 79).

These actions may include:

✓ adding boy-friendly resources;

✓ modelling how to use and access resources;

✓ redesigning the area and the wider provision;

✓ repeating the survey to monitor the impact of the changes introduced.

Systems

Boys tend to respond positively to systems. They need things to be ordered and systematic. They need the security of knowing where to go and where to look and to have the confidence to know that what they are looking for will be where they expected it to be. If this doesn't happen regularly then they are likely to give up and become frustrated and consequently their learning will be limited.

Therefore, there should be high standards of tidiness, order and cleanliness in your setting. All resources and furniture must be maintained to a high level of good repair. To ensure this happens, a written schedule of cleaning, repair and replenishment should be implemented.

Helping boys become confident, competent and above all independent learners has to be a high priority in all settings. The checklist 'Enabling learning environments', on page 80, provides the elements required in an enabling learning environment and will help you to ensure that this is possible.

Remember!
The quality of the learning environment has a major impact on the quality of learning.

To effectively support boys' learning, staff need to understand how boys learn and value what they respond to appropriately. The checklist 'Roll of staff in supporting boys' learning', on page 57 can be used as a tool to encourage reflection and discussion.

Remember!
When boys feel valued and cared for they will learn more.

A teacher observed that a boy was having difficulty understanding the value of numbers. She used Compare Bears to teach this concept. The boy did not engage with the activity. Later in the day the boy was outdoors playing with pine cones. She repeated the number activity. In this context the boy was instantly engaged.

At a parents' consultation evening, a teacher commented to a boy's parents that he was failing to engage with phonics. Further discussion revealed that at home he had built a fuse box from cardboard, wire and pipe cleaners. The teacher used this knowledge of his interests to engage him in phonics. They created a 'special phonics box' with letters that could be pulled up and down on strings.

Discuss...
Do adults continually reflect on practice and implement change based on boys' observed interests and fascinations?

Discuss...
Are the indoor and outdoor learning environments given equal value? Do boys access areas of continuous provision (indoors and outdoors) independently?

Discuss...
Do boys demonstrate an understanding of organisational systems?

Do boys initiate activities, show initiative and make decisions?

Discuss...
Does the outdoor provision extend boys' learning and provide opportunities that are not so readily available indoors?

Share your thoughts and feelings, what other examples have you observed?

Review your planning

Use the planning checklist *'Does planning take into account how boys learn?'*, on page 82 as a useful tool.

Review your daily routine using the daily routine checklist *'After observing boys completing self-chosen activities'*, on page 83.

Final questions and actions for practitioners

- Do we plan experiences for boys that builds on their interests and fascinations? If the answer is 'no' or 'not enough', what are we going to do about it?

- Do we value boys' strengths as active learners and problem solvers? If the answer is 'no', or 'not enough', what are we going to do about it?

- Do we expect boys to be compliant, passive recipients of new skills and knowledge? If the answer is 'yes', what do we need to do?

- Are resources and displays full of positive images that do not stereotype along gender lines? If the answer is 'no' or 'not enough', what are we going to do about it?

- Are resources accessible in such a way that boys and girls are likely to use them? If the answer is 'no' or 'not enough', what are we going to do about it?

chapter 9

Partnership with parents

This chapter specifically focuses on how to work with parents to try and ensure that their sons don't underachieve in school. By raising their awareness, reducing their anxiety and engaging them in practical activities, we can have a positive impact upon the development of boys in our setting and help close the gender gap.

Research indicates that children whose parents take an active involvement in their education tend to perform better at school that those who don't. Practitioners, however, will often feel frustrated by the fact that some parents seem to have lower expectations of their son than of their daughter. On many occasions practitioners may feel that their work in the setting is somewhat undermined or even totally devalued as a result.

▶ *A young nursery teacher recounted the story of a parent with whom she had what the teacher felt was a necessary discussion about the boy, only for the parent to say, 'Don't worry love, when you've had children of your own I'm sure you'll understand.'*

▶ *It's not uncommon for parents to have completely different perceptions of their son at home to the practitioners' views of the boy in nursery. One practitioner cited an example of a mother who would frequently moan about how her boy 'ruled the roost' at home whilst in nursery he was well behaved all day.*

Many nurseries and schools find it hard to engage parents in their child's education. When a setting or school holds an educational session for parents, very often the parents they would really like to attend are the ones who don't turn up. We need to enhance our efforts to get parents engaged in their child's learning. The parent sheets at the back of this book can be used to plan an educational session for parents. You may also find the information in the following section a useful template for organising and delivering a series of effective parents' sessions.

Boys and girls: getting it right from the start

The purpose of the sessions

The sessions have been developed to increase parent's understanding of how important it is to encourage children to become independent and to support them in their learning. It provides parents with practical ideas and strategies to support children's learning through everyday activities within the home and local environment. Research has shown that from an early age there is a gap between boys' and girls' achievement. The sessions are designed to address this issue by providing strategies that will raise achievement in all children but with a particular emphasis on helping parents to raise boys' achievement.

Session content

There are four sessions, each lasting 1 hour 30 minutes:

Session 1: **Understanding boys and girls**

Session 2: **Learning through the senses**

Session 3: **Taking the pressure off**

Session 4: **Developing confidence and self-belief**

When working with parents remember:

Prepare your room:

- Ensure it is clean and tidy

- It is a comfortable temperature

- There are enough chairs of the correct size

- Arrange chairs and tables in an informal position

It is a good idea to prepare hand-outs and materials before each session. Remember to have extra copies ready in case additional parents decide to attend unexpectedly.

Refreshments should be prepared before the session begins. In a school, you might ask year six boys to do the refreshments. You could take this further by engaging them in the session too!

Materials

✓ Activity plan for each session

✓ Notes to support the delivery of each session

✓ Hand-outs that can be taken home

✓ Question and answer cards

✓ A plastic wallet for each course participant

Session 1 | Understanding boys and girls

Objectives of the session

- Develop a clearer understanding of how society reacts to boys and girls

- Understand the need to help children to develop impulse control

- Understand the importance of developing children's independence

Outcome

- Be aware of the negative messages that clothing and merchandise can give

- Parents have strategies to help their children to manage impulse control

- Parents practically encourage the development of independence within the home

Time	Activity	Materials and hand-outs
15 minutes	ICE BREAKER	Two sets of playing cards List of questions Large sheets of paper
15 minutes	SHARING THE DATA RELATING TO BOY'S AND GIRL'S ACHIEVEMENT DEVELOPING INDEPENDENCE	National data • EYFSP • SATS • GCSE 'Developing independence' hand-out page
15 minutes	LABELLING ACTIVITY • Sort photographs of clothing by gender • Sort gender-biased items • Give out one marshmallow to each course participant	Photographs of children's clothing Gender biased items Marshmallows
15 minutes	BREAK	Refreshments
10 minutes	PLAY THE MARSHMALLOW GAME	Marshmallows
15 minutes	INDEPENDENCE SKILLS QUESTION AND ANSWER SESSION STRATEGIES TO SUPPORT TIDYING UP	'Q&A Card 1', page 73 Laundry basket and a selection of socks
5 minutes	SUMMARY OF SESSION • Share the focus for the next session • Give out take home hand-out	'Activities to help with dressing' sheet, page 72

Guidance notes

Session 1: Understanding boys and girls

ICE BREAKER

Pair identical cards from two packs of playing cards (only use enough for the number of participants, e.g. five sets of identical cards for ten participants).

Before the session, give these out randomly: one for each participant.

On a large sheet of paper write the following questions:

- **What is your name?**

- **What are the names and ages of your children?**

- **What is your favourite colour?**

- **Tell me something unusual about yourself.**

Ask participants to find the person holding the matching card to their's. Explain that the purpose of the activity is to introduce their partner to the group. Participants ask their partners the questions on the sheet of paper. Before returning to their seats they must introduce their partner to the group.

SHARING THE DATA RELATING TO BOYS' AND GIRLS' ACHIEVEMENT

Before the session, become familiar with your school and national data. This is available from:

www.gov.uk/government/organisations/department-for-education/about/statistics

You could use your school's data and national data information to form the basis of a question and answer session. Begin with the 'end picture,' e.g. 'Who do you think performs best in GSCE mathematics – boys or girls?' Then share Foundation Stage data and point out the gender gap. At this point it would be useful to demonstrate that the school/ setting is aware of the gender gap and has begun to make changes as a result – you could even list some of the changes already in place. You also need to stress, however, that 'We can't do it without you!'

DEVELOPING INDEPENDENCE

Photocopy 'Q&A Card 1: Developing independence' (page 73)

Hand out the sheet and discuss the cycle of dependence. What can we do to break the cycle?

LABELLING ACTIVITY

- Print photographs of children's clothing from the Internet (e.g. T-shirt with 'Here comes trouble' or 'Mummy's Little Princess').

- Collect items that demonstrate gender bias, e.g. pencil cases or car stickers.

- Hand out photographs of boy's and girl's clothing and gender-biased items.

- With the person next to them, participants sort photographs and items into positive and negative categories.

Notes
The photographs of the clothing and the items are gender biased. Many participants may think slogans such as, 'Mummy's Little Princess,' create a positive image. Participants may think that the slogan, 'Boys are stupid – throw rocks at them', to be funny. As early years leaders, these views need to be gently challenged. Discuss the impact that the constant reinforcement of the labelling has on the child's self-esteem. Children begin to believe the sentiments expressed by the labels and may demonstrate this in their behaviours.

PLAY THE MARSHMALLOW GAME

- Buy enough marshmallows for each participant to have two. Before break-time give one marshmallow to each participant and give them the following instruction: 'You can eat the marshmallow now, but if you wait until after break-time, you will get another one later'.

- After break-time give an additional marshmallow to those who have not eaten their first marshmallow.

Notes

Explain the research. Children were given a marshmallow and told that they could eat it now or wait while the researcher did a little job outside the room. If they waited and didn't eat the marshmallow, on his return they would be given another one.

Research showed that the children who ate the marshmallow and did not wait had limited impulse control at an early age. They did not achieve as high academically and socially as the children who waited for a second marshmallow. Stress the importance of helping children to develop impulse control and self-regulation. For example, if a child asks for a drink, don't stop what you are doing and respond instantly. Talk to the child and say, 'I will get you a drink when I finish this.' Ask parents if they can provide other, similar examples.

INDEPENDENCE SKILLS QUESTION AND ANSWER SESSION

Resources

- Laundry basket

- Socks

- Q&A Card 1: Developing independence

Notes

Read out the first question. While demonstrating how to sort laundry from the basket, discuss how involving the child in simple household tasks promotes independence and offers a range of learning opportunities. Read out the other questions on the sheet. Give participants time to think about their answers. If there is time, discuss this as a group. Give out a copy of 'Q&A Card 1' to each participant.

STRATEGIES TO SUPPORT TIDYING UP

Resources

- Prepare a basket of Duplo™ with a corresponding digital photograph of the Duplo™ attached to it.

- Show the basket of Duplo™ to participants.

- Ask participants to consider how they organise their children's toys and help children to tidy up by themselves:

  ★ Organise toys by type

  ★ Limit the amount of toys to which children have free access

  ★ Use digital photographs to support tidying up.

Notes

When asking a child to tidy up, give short simple instructions. If you ask a child to tidy their bedroom, they may not know where to begin. Instead, support the child by asking them to pick up the cars and put the away. Then ask them to pick up the play people and put them away. Then ask them to pick up their pyjamas and put them under their pillow.

SUMMARY OF THE SESSION

- Photocopy the 'Activities to help with dressing' sheet, page 72.

- Summarise the main points from the session:

  ★ Gap between girls' and boys' achievement

  ★ Labelling

  ★ Impulse control

  ★ Promoting independence

  ★ Share focus for next session – Learning through the senses.

Session 2 | Learning through the senses

Objectives of the session

- Investigate different methods of learning

- Understand the importance of active learning

- Support participants to understand how they can engage children in learning

Outcome

- Participants evaluate their own interaction with their children

- Participants plan active learning opportunities

Time	Activity	Materials and hand-outs
15 minutes	ICE BREAKER	List of information to find Paper, pencil Small prize Large sheets of paper
15 minutes	FORMAL LEARNING ACTIVITY You may also use your own examples to demonstrate different methods of learning	Worksheet: 'The life cycle of a butterfly', page 84, glue, scissors, coloured pencils.
15 minutes	JELLY BABY ACTIVITY	Jelly Babies Photograph of a Jelly Baby Words 'Jelly Baby' on card Pens Large sheets of paper
15 minutes	BREAK	Refreshments
25 minutes	MAKE A PRAISE POSTCARD	Coloured card Glue Selection of resources that are available in the home and garden such as pasta, leaves, wrapping paper Containers for holding resources
5 minutes	SUMMARY OF SESSION • **Give out hand-outs that can be taken home** • **Share the focus for the next session**	Recipe for play dough, page 86

BOYS WILL BE BRILLIANT!

Guidance notes

Session 2 Learning through the senses

ICE BREAKER

On a sheet of paper write:

- Find someone who has a red car

- Find someone who is wearing a necklace

- Find someone who plays sport

- Find someone who has been on holiday to Spain

- Find someone who dislikes chocolate

(Provide paper and pencil for those who wish to make notes)

> **Notes**
> Participants ask each other questions to find out information relating to the questions above. The group then feeds back verbally. The winner (the person who finds people to match the most questions) receives a small prize.
>
> Before the session begins, summarise the previous session. You could encourage one of the participants to do this too. At this point it would be good to share any positive outcomes of the previous session. You might like to begin with a discussion around parents' experiences of how their sons learn at home and the things they say they enjoy doing at school.

FORMAL ACTIVITY

- Photocopy the worksheet 'The life cycle of a butterfly', page 84. Set out glue, scissors and coloured pencils.

> **Notes**
> Participants work independently to complete the worksheet. Explain they only have 15 minutes to finish this activity. While participants are busy, walk around the tables and make comments about what you observe. When the time is up ask the participants what they have learnt from the activity.
>
> The purpose of this activity is to help participants to experience a formal learning situation. You will help participants explore how they felt and what they learned during the activity.

JELLY BABY ACTIVITY

- Place on each table: a bowl of Jelly Babies, a sheet of paper, a pen, a photograph of a Jelly Baby and the written words, Jelly Baby.

- Divide participants into groups of four. Ask them to discuss and write down five facts about the Jelly Babies. Emphasise that there are no right or wrong answers. Take feedback from each group in turn.

- Ask them to write these words on a large sheet of paper. Identify words that involve the senses, e.g. stretchy, sweet. Remember to emphasise that this activity should be enjoyable and non-threatening.

- Show the photograph of the Jelly Baby. Ask: if they had no previous knowledge of a Jelly Baby, what they could learn from it? Refer to the list they have just written and circle the words that they can learn from the photograph.

Repeat the process with the written words, Jelly Baby.

> **Notes**
> Refer to the formal activity on page 84. Would participants have learnt more if they had explored caterpillars and butterflies? Stress the importance of active learning. In order to learn actively, children need to act upon materials, they need to manipulate materials, they need choice, and they need to be supported by staff so that they begin to articulate their learning.

MAKING A PRAISE POSTCARD

- Prepare materials: coloured card, glue and other resources that you have collected.

- Divide up the resources into containers, make sure there are enough in each for four participants.

- Ask participants to use the resources to make a praise postcard. Encourage participants to write sentences such as 'I'm so proud of you'.

> **Notes**
> Support participants and highlight the learning that has taken place and encourages participants to discuss how they felt as they took part in these activities. Model how you support and encourage learning.

SUMMARY OF THE SESSION

- Photocopy the recipe for play dough, page 86.

- Summarise the main points from the session:

  ★ Children learn best through first-hand experience

  ★ Children learn through their senses as they play and manipulate objects and materials

  ★ Children learn when they are in a non-threatening environment

  ★ Staff need to support children's learning rather than dominate and direct the learning

- Share the focus for next session: Taking the pressure off

Session 3 Taking the pressure off

Objectives of the session

- Understand the importance of telling stories

- Help participants to understand the writing process.

- Teach participants to recognise opportunities for mathematical development in their home and local environments

Outcome

- Participants use everyday situations to tell stories to their children

- Participants plan to support the development of fine motor and mathematical skills through practical experiences

Time	Activity	Materials and hand-outs
15 minutes	ICE BREAKER	Storytelling cards
15 minutes	READING A STORY	Book: *Kipper's Toybox* by Mick Inkpen.
20 minutes	WRITING IS MORE THAN HOLDING A PENCIL	'Writing is more than holding a pencil and making marks', page 76 Bubble wrap Tea bags Paper plates Scarves Bottles of bubbles
15 minutes	BREAK	Refreshments
20 minutes	MATHS AROUND THE HOME	Large sheet of paper, pen and 'Maths around the home' sheet, page 85
5 minutes	SUMMARY OF SESSION 'Q&A Cards 3 & 4' Share the focus for the next session	'Q&A Cards 3 & 4', pages 77 and 78

Guidance notes

Session 3 | Taking the pressure off

Before the session begins, summarise the previous session. You could encourage a willing participant to do this too. At this point it would also be good to share the positive outcomes of previous sessions.

ICE BREAKER

- Make three sets of storytelling cards. Give a set to each group of participants.

- Participants use the storytelling cards to tell a story.

STORY READING

- Familiarise yourself with the book, *Kipper's Toybox* by Mick Inkpen.

Draw attention to:

★ The illustrations

★ The fact that children know all about toys

★ How the story is simple and easy to understand

★ The mouse on every page

★ The mathematical content of the story

★ How the size of the writing dictates how the storyteller should read the words.

Notes

Research has shown how important it is that children have books read to them from an early age. This is particularly important for boys as they often prefer non-fiction. In order to be good writers, children need to internalise the pattern of stories. All children – but particularly boys – ideally need to read with or be read to by older males, as well as women, in the close or extended family. Seeing older males reading in their home environment help to motivate children's own reading.

Read *Kipper's Toybox* to participants. Use the notes above to generate discussion. Suggest to participants that they join the local library and read appropriate stories regularly to their children.

WRITING IS MORE THAN HOLDING A PENCIL

- Photocopy page 76 'Writing is more than holding a pencil and making marks'.

- Place the resources on the table. Each group of four participants should have:

  ★ One piece of bubble wrap

  ★ One paper plate with tea leaves

  ★ One scarf

  ★ One bottle of bubbles

- Ask the participants to explore the materials. Use the notes here to facilitate discussion.

Notes

Remind parents of the issues around late development of fine motor skills in boys, the implications this has on their self-esteem and confidence, particularly when they feel under pressure to write neatly.

By exploring the materials above, participants are developing their fine motor skills. Playing with the tea leaves provides the opportunity for them to make marks. Popping bubble wrap strengthens their pincer grip. Catching scarves and bubbles strengthens the muscles in the arms and develops hand-eye coordination. All of these movements are a prerequisite to children holding a writing implement and using it to make marks.

Emphasise the importance of providing opportunities (indoor and outdoor) for the children – especially boys – to explore movement in preparation for writing. Tell the participants that if we miss out this stage and expect children to write using a pencil before they are physically ready, the 'seeds of boys' underachievement can be sown in the early years.' (Marjory Overy).

Give out copies of 'Writing is more than holding a pencil and making marks', page 76. Ask participants to read it during the break.

MATHS AROUND THE HOME

- Set out a large sheet of paper and pen. Copy 'Maths around the home', page 85, onto the paper.

- There are opportunities all around us to develop mathematical skills. If possible, give an example from the room in which you are working. For example, you could talk about the shape of the windows, the number of chairs in the room, etc.

- Give each group of four participants an area of the home/garden e.g. garden, bathroom, kitchen.

- Ask participants to consider what opportunities there are for developing mathematical skills within each of these areas.

- Write the name of each area on the paper. Take ideas from each group.

- Give out the 'Maths around the home' hand-outs and discuss. Suggest participants choose one activity to try at home with their child.

- Summary of the session

- Copy 'Q&A Cards 3 & 4' (pages 77 and 78)

SUMMARY OF THE SESSION

- Parents need to tell and read stories to their children

- Children need to develop listening and storytelling skills

- Writing is more than holding a pencil

- Exploiting the many learning opportunities within the home

- Share focus for next session – confident communicators

- Give out the 'Question and answer cards' hand-out

Session 4 Developing confidence and self-belief

Objectives of the session

- Understand the importance of talking about and naming feelings and emotions

- Support participants to understand how positive reinforcement generates confidence and self-esteem

- Support participants to develop strategies to foster effective communication

Outcome

- Participants use everyday situations to talk about their feelings and emotions

- Participants are proactive in using positive language to build children's confidence

Time	Activity	Materials and hand-outs
15 minutes	ICE BREAKER • **Demonstration of self-belief** • **Visualisation**	
15 minutes	DO WE TALK TO BOYS AND GIRLS DIFFERENTLY?	Words to describe a baby written on cards
10 minutes	QUESTION AND ANSWER CARD	'Q&A Card 2', page 74
20 minutes	MAKE EMOTION CARDS	Coloured card, scissors, felt-tipped pens
15 minutes	BREAK	Refreshments
20 minutes	VERBAL INSTRUCTIONS	Individual sheets of paper, pencils

Guidance notes

Session 4 Developing confidence and self-belief

ICE BREAKER
Demonstration of self-belief

- Ask for a volunteer. The volunteer stands where all participants can see them. Ask the volunteer, 'What is your name?' The volunteer is asked to put their arm straight out and confidently keep repeating 'My name is......'. The trainer attempts to push the volunteer's hand down towards the floor.

Note: it should be difficult to push the volunteer's arm down. You will feel the resistance.

- Find out something that the volunteer cannot do well. For example, can you sing? Can you salsa? The volunteer is asked to put their arm straight out in front and say repeatedly in a dejected voice 'I can't sing'—the other participants give sympathetic verbal responses, e.g. 'ah never mind'. The trainer attempts to push the arm towards the floor.

Note: it should be easier to push the arm down. Explain to the participants that lack of self-belief affects the whole body.

DO WE TALK TO BOYS AND GIRLS DIFFERENTLY?

- Prepare a list of words that can be used to describe babies. Write these words on cards, e.g. happy, contented, noisy, delightful, and unsettled. Make a set of word cards for each participant.

- Participants sort the word cards by gender. Which words would they use when talking to or about a male baby or female baby? Use the notes below to guide your discussion.

Notes
In most Western societies, adults speak differently to boys from birth. I was watching educational professionals holding and talking to one another about three-week-old twins, one female the other male. I observed that the language used was gender specific. The male child was described as 'big, a bouncer, a bruiser' the female child was described as 'beautiful, precious, gorgeous'. (Tallent, 2008)

Compared to girls, boys are exposed to more vigorous 'rough and tumble' play by males with different accompanying language ('fatherese'). (Opal Dunn, 2003)

Children develop their gender identity (knowing whether they are male or female) by the age of three. As boys get older many of them think that in school, teachers prefer girls and the evidence they cite is that, for example, teachers don't shout at girls!

VISUALISATION

- Participants stand in a space: they extend their arm and point forwards. They remain stationary while rotating their upper body and arm as far as they can behind them (towards the right if using right arm/towards left if using left arm). Note where there finger is now pointing.

- Participants return to their starting position. The trainer then asks all participants to close their eyes and says 'imagine your arm going to the point you reached before but this time you don't stop—you keep going right round'. The trainer then asks all participants to open their eyes, put their arm forward and try again.

Notes
The second time, participants should point further than they did in the first instance. Explain to the participants that when children hear what they need to do, they can visualise and this helps them to succeed. When we hear ourselves say that we can't do something then that often becomes reality, whereas if we feel positive and rehearse success in our heads, we are more likely to achieve success.

Before the session begins, summarise the previous session. You could encourage a willing participant to do this too. At this point it would also be good to share any positive outcomes that resulted from the previous sessions.

QUESTION AND ANSWER CARD

Photocopy 'Q&A Card 2' (page 74)

- Read out the questions and ask participants to answer them. Discuss their answers and then read out the answers on the card.

MAKE EMOTION CARDS

Use the notes below as a framework for discussing the importance of supporting children's emotional well-being:

- Some researchers maintain that boys may not develop a full capacity for emotional depth. Parents – and in particular fathers or other males within the family – play a significant role in supporting boys' emotional development. A father who tells a young boy not to cry or urges him to 'man up', may well inhibit that child's ability to deal with greater losses later in his life.

- Dr. Harriett Lerner suggests that 'Boys are still taught to toughen up, to deny vulnerability, and not to ask for emotional comfort from other males'. (The Mother Dance, 1999) As a result, some boys are less able than girls to deal with the emotional upheavals that accompany adolescence. Recent statistics show that teenage boys are five times more likely to commit suicide. It is often argued that adult males who lacked emotional development as a boy struggle to develop healthy relationships.

- Boys tend to focus their attention on objects and activity, whereas girls tend to focus their attention on people and communication.

- According to psychologists at the University of Cambridge in England, boys prefer to watch mechanical motion over human motion. Simon Baron-Cohen and his team at the University of Cambridge found that among one-year-old children who were given a choice of films to watch, the girls look longer at the cover or poster of a film that features a human face, while boys were more interested in films featuring cars. He concludes that girls tend to be nature's empathisers whilst boys tend to be nature's systemisers (Baron-Cohen, 2003 The Essential Difference).

- To support emotional well-being, all children – and boys in particular – need staff who give them:

  ★ Frequent encouragement to complete a task successfully

  ★ Ways to resolve conflicts

  ★ Names for emotions

  ★ Emotional and physical comfort

  ★ Justified praise and specific praise, e.g. 'Aren't you clever, I love the way you have drawn the face and included all the detail. This stimulates and develops their self-esteem.

At this point it would be useful to ask parents how they manage to get their child to express their feelings. In what circumstance do they find it relatively easy to get their child to express their feelings?

- Cut circles from coloured card, at least three circles per participant. Provide a selection of felt-tipped pens.

- Participants use felt-tipped pens to draw a face on a circle of card with an emotion or expression on it. Tell participants if they are drawing the emotion 'happy,' to draw what they see on a happy face (big smile and bright eyes).

> ### Notes
> If parents have children under three, they should limit the face cards to three main emotions: cross, sad and happy. If children are aged three or older, start off with the three face cards (cross, sad and happy) and add more, such as anxious, frustrated, surprised, and scared.
>
> Tell participants that these face cards can be used to gauge children's knowledge of different emotions. Use the cards to begin a conversation about how a child feels. Use the corresponding words for the emotions that the child describes. This gives children the language to help them express their emotions verbally.

VERBAL INSTRUCTIONS

- Some children feel confused and frustrated because they cannot communicate effectively with staff and other children. This can be manifested in the child's behaviour.

- Share with participants strategies to support children to communicate effectively. Use the notes below. Show participants written examples of inappropriate instructions and explanations. Read together. Ask participants to rephrase them.

- Wherever possible, use visual clues (pictures, objects, gestures etc.) to support understanding:

  ★ Speak slowly and clearly

  ★ Emphasise the key words

  ★ Repeat the instruction or explanation

  ★ Emphasise facial expression

  ★ Break verbal instructions into manageable chunks, e.g. say 'pick up the cars. Put them in the box.' Rather than just 'tidy your toys'.

- Demonstrate wherever possible

- Check that the child understands what to do

- Do not put pressure on the child to respond verbally

- Remember:

  ★ Try to use suggestions rather than commands

  ★ Try to use positive rather than negative comments

  ★ Try to encourage and praise rather than discourage and criticise

In pairs, participants should practise giving instructions to each other.

SUMMARY OF THE SESSION

Summarise the main points from the session:

- Consider how you talk to boys and girls

- How to support effective communication

- Importance of naming emotions

- Positive touch is vitally important in developing children's self-esteem and sense of emotional well-being

You might like to ask for volunteers to help you turn the ideas behind, and the outcomes from, these sessions into a useful leaflet for other parents'.

Celebration of course: each trainer to plan individually.

Attitude checklist

Reflect on your own practice to complete the following check list.

Supportive interaction	Non-supportive interactions
Adults establish clear expectations of the positive attitudes and behaviours that they want to see.	Adults focus on misbehaviour, constantly correct boys and compare them with the girls or each other in a negative way. Adults constantly say 'Do this or do not do that'. *Clearly unhelpful as this will often result in undesired behaviour. The brain cannot process the words 'don't' 'not' or 'no'.* *Try this– do not think of pink elephants – whatever you do, do not think of pink elephants. Did you manage it?*
Adults respond positively to boys' needs and questions.	Adults talk down to boys. Adults stop listening – at this point boys will stop communicating.
Adults kneel down and talk quietly to boys. (Boys particularly like adults to relate to them 'at their level'.)	Adults raise their voices and shout at boys across the room. *Boys will often see this as teachers preferring girls to boys – 'They don't shout at girls, because they don't want to make them cry! But they shout at boys!'* *I asked one boy, 'Why do you think they shout at boys?'* *He said, 'Because they think we're stronger.'* *'Well aren't you?' I asked, mischievously* *'Well… on the outside, maybe,' he said, 'on the outside'.*
Adults encourage boys to work without constant adult intervention.	Adults present solutions without allowing boys enough thinking time. How do you stop a boy from thinking? Tell him the answer!
Adults provide appropriate challenges.	Adults set tasks that are undemanding.

Boys Will Be Brilliant! published by Featherstone © Linda Tallent and Gary Wilson

Activities to help with dressing

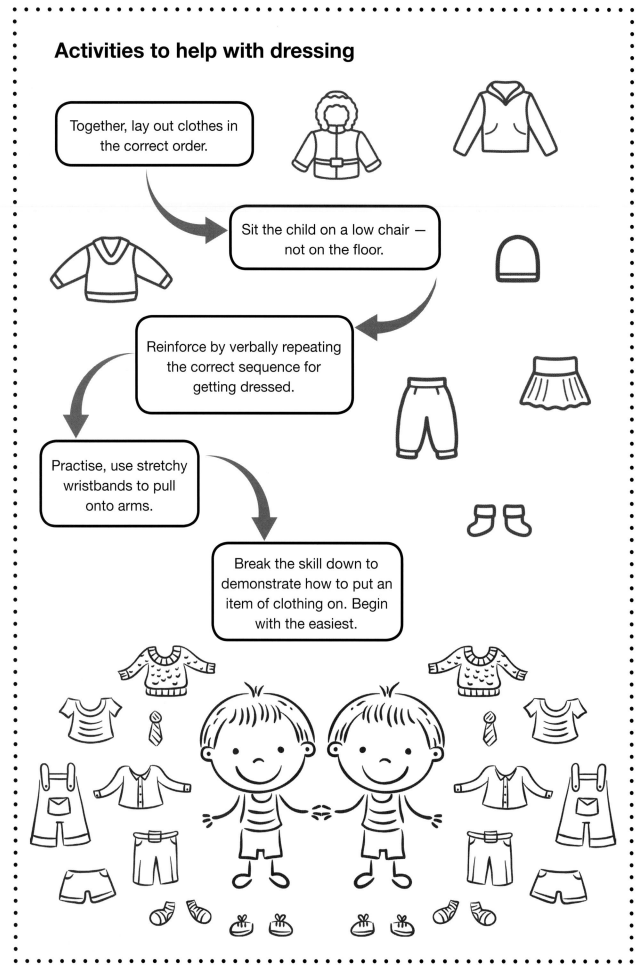

Together, lay out clothes in the correct order.

Sit the child on a low chair — not on the floor.

Reinforce by verbally repeating the correct sequence for getting dressed.

Practise, use stretchy wristbands to pull onto arms.

Break the skill down to demonstrate how to put an item of clothing on. Begin with the easiest.

Q&A Card 1: Developing independence

Remember to start with a limited choice of tasks and then steadily increase the number.

Question	Boy	Girl	Answer
Do you encourage your child to help around the house?			If not, encourage them to help with sorting washing into colours, socks into pairs, etc.
Do you encourage your child to dress themselves?			If not, then begin by encouraging them to choose what type of clothes to wear, discussing the practicalities of their choice.
Do you encourage your child to help prepare meals?			If not, then make setting the table a joint activity: counting and sorting cutlery and laying the correct number of places.
Do you encourage your child to help tidy things away after meals?			If not, then ask for help with returning items to the correct places in the cupboards or fridge.

Boys Will Be Brilliant! published by Featherstone © Linda Tallent and Gary Wilson

Q&A Card 2: Supporting emotional development

Remember: the more you talk about a wide range of emotions, the quicker children will develop empathy.

Question	Boy	Girl	Answer
Does your child have words to describe the way they feel?			Make different facial expressions and ask them to name the feeling. You could use a series of photos of your own family acting these out which may be even more effective!
Do you talk about feelings to your child? Love? Sadness? Fear? Anger?			According to research, there can be a tendency for us to talk far more to young girls about these emotions and for us to be more likely to talk only about fear and anger with boys. Pay attention to what you do and adapt if necessary. We need to honour young girls' and young boys' tender feelings.
Do you frequently cuddle your child, for example when reading to them?			Positive touch is a hugely important part of developing young children's self-esteem and sense of emotional well-being. More hugs please!
Do you talk about the importance of caring about: Themselves? Others? The environment? Pets?			If, for example, you need to discourage them from trampling plants in your garden, planting plants together could work as quite an deterrent because they will feel a sense of ownership and responsibility over the garden.

Boys Will Be Brilliant! published by Featherstone © Linda Tallent and Gary Wilson

Taking the pressure off

It doesn't matter if he can't hold a pencil yet. But it would help if he could develop fine motor skills.

It doesn't matter if he can't write his name yet. But it would help if he could recognise his name.

It doesn't matter if he can't read books yet. But it would help if he were read to, was excited by stories, could retell stories and join in with chants from familiar stories.

It doesn't matter if he can't draw a recognisable picture yet. But it would help if he could use materials to draw circles and lines.

It doesn't matter if he can't recognise the letters of the alphabet yet. But it would help if he could hear the initial letter sounds in words.

Taking the pressure off

Boys Will Be Brilliant! published by Featherstone © Linda Tallent and Gary Wilson

Writing is more than holding a pencil and making marks

You need to start BIG!

Provide scarves, ribbons, bubbles. Encourage the boys to catch the bubbles and to make patterns by twirling ribbons and scarves.

Provide decorating brushes and buckets of water. Encourage the boys to paint the walls and fences.

Provide low level climbing activities and planks to walk across.

Provide open cardboard boxes to crawl though.

Many of the activities that help children to learn to write do not actually involve children in writing:

Provide newspaper, tissue paper for scrunching up and bubble wrap for popping.

Provide dough that can be rolled, cut, pounded and pinched.

Provide dried beans, pasta, lentils and rice for transferring into containers using a spoon, tweezers or index finger and thumb.

Provide a thin layer of sand in a shallow tray. Use index finger to make patterns and shapes.

Provide a selection of plastic jars with screw top lids, children must open them to find the hidden treasure.

Provide squeezy bottles filled with water: make patterns on the ground.

Q&A Card 3: Supporting early literacy development

Remember: too much pressure at an early age can create later literacy difficulties.

Question	Boy	Girl	Answer
Is your child interested in words?			If not, try to get them to identify letters in their own name wherever they occur, especially in places that might interest them. For example, you might point out a letter on a sign that is the same as a letter in their name. Encourage children to read environmental print, for example brand or shop names.
Do older females and males read to your child?			Having adults read to children supports them in developing language and literacy skills, but boys will especially benefit from having male family members read to them. It is also helpful if boys can see older males reading for their own pleasure and enjoyment in the home.
Do you read mostly fiction to your child?			Start by reading stories with repeating patterns first to engage. **TOP TIPS** 1. Carry on reading, even if.... • They switch off half way through • They start getting restless and fiddling around • They get up and walk away. (You could even walk around the room yourself acting the story out.... Go on, try it!) 2. Many boys like stories: • With humour • That appeal to their sense of mischief • That link to their culture (media characters for example) • That are slightly scary.

Boys Will Be Brilliant! published by Featherstone © Linda Tallent and Gary Wilson

Q&A Card 4: Supporting early literacy development

Remember: too much pressure at an early age can create later literacy difficulties.

Question	Boy	Girl	Answer
Do you read mostly non-fiction?			Boys really need to read fiction in order to help them develop imagination, comprehension and reflective skills. Reflection is often the weakest part of their learning process.
Do you take every opportunity you can to develop your child's speaking and listening skills?			Name and categorise things you see together whilst out and about (e.g. 'Can we find any red vegetables in the shop?' 'What do you call this vegetable? — a tomato'). Say out loud what you are about to do and why you are about to do it (e.g. 'We need to wash the car. It's very dirty. We need a bucket. Where do we keep the bucket? etc.).
Do you make up and tell stories for your child? Do you sit around the table for meals and talk?			Make up stories about everyday activities but add an exciting twist. This will help to develop children's listening skills and encourage them to ask questions. When conversation takes place around the table, children learn to listen and take turns, making use of the vocabulary they have learned. This can provide opportunities to make small corrections in their language (Child: 'I runned down the hill.' Adult: 'Yes, you ran down the hill! Was it fun?')

Boys Will Be Brilliant! published by Featherstone © Linda Tallent and Gary Wilson

Observation survey

Classroom Areas (possible focus: gender, passive/active, use of resources)

Class: _____   Date: _____   Number of pupils: _____

Completed by: _____

Areas of the indoor and outdoor learning environment	1st sample	2nd sample	3rd sample	4th sample

What they are going to do next:

Boys Will Be Brilliant! published by Featherstone © Linda Tallent and Gary Wilson

Complete the following checklist:

Enabling learning environment	
Is there a system in place whereby each member of staff is assigned to a specific area of the learning environment to resource, maintain and keep clean?	
Are resources re-stocked so that the appropriate amount of provision is in place for the children to access at all times?	
Are floors clear at the end of each day?	
Are all surfaces cleared/sorted at the end of each day?	
Are all resources appropriately labelled to include the photograph/name/number of resources on labels? Ensure photographs of resources clearly match labels.	
Are areas over stocked? Be selective about the resources that are needed for learning and rotate the stock so that the range is accessible – this can be done over time.	
Are resources that are not to be accessed by children stored elsewhere to preserve the quality of continuous provision and the learning environment?	
Are all resources that are to be accessed by children easily and safely accessible to allow for independent use and ease of use?	
Are teachers' documentation/resources neatly organised and stored with only the essential stored on show?	

Boys Will Be Brilliant! published by Featherstone © Linda Tallent and Gary Wilson

Complete the following checklist:

Role of staff in supporting boys' learning	
Do staff recognise when it is appropriate to engage boys in self-initiated activities to challenge and extend children's thinking so that learning is taken forward?	
Do staff talk with boys about what they plan to do and how they will do it?	
Do staff encourage and support boys to work co-operatively, without taking over or directing?	
Do staff promote 'good' behaviour and teach boys how to take care of themselves and behave appropriately?	
Are staff responsive and supportive of boys' emotional needs and do they promote acceptance of each other's differences?	
Do staff support boys to evaluate what they did well and what they would change next time?	
Do staff record boys' interests and strengths to identify the next learning steps?	
Do all staff working in the early years contribute to the observation, assessment, recording and planning process?	
Do staff effectively model language to extend boys' speaking and comprehension skills?	
Do staff ensure there is a balance of adult-led, adult-guided and child–initiated activities indoors and outdoors?	
Are planned activities multi-sensory, active and play-based, well-planned and purposeful?	
Are assessment for learning opportunities maximised with boys actively involved?	
Do routines support children to be effective and motivated learners?	

Boys Will Be Brilliant! published by Featherstone © Linda Tallent and Gary Wilson

Planning checklist
Does planning take into account how boys learn?

Complete the following checklist:

Opportunities to work in a variety of groupings.	Comment	No opportunities to work in a variety of groupings.	Comment
Activities are play based and focus on building upon children's previous learning and interests.		Activities focus on cognitive development and rote learning.	
Tasks are differentiated.		All boys expected to complete the same task together.	
Adult-led activities are purposeful and engage boys.		Adult-led activities are not purposeful.	
Adults interact with boys to facilitate their use of materials, e.g. adding new materials when needed and making suggestions to extend boys' play.		Activities that are directed by the adult tend to be product orientated.	
There is a 'purposeful buzz' from boys.		Boys are encouraged to be passive and quiet.	

Boys Will Be Brilliant! published by Featherstone © Linda Tallent and Gary Wilson

Daily routine checklist
After observing boys completing self-chosen activities

Complete the following checklist:

	Comment		Comment
Boys know the daily routine, visual strategies are used.		Boys are unsure of the daily routine.	
Boys know what is expected of them during child-initiated and adult-guided learning.		Boys are unsure of the expectations during child-initiated and adult-guided learning.	
A balance of adult-led, adult-guided and child initiated activities.		Over emphasis on adult-led, adult-guided, or child-initiated activities.	
Sufficient time for boys to select own activities and play for an extended time.		Insufficient time for boys to select own activities and play for an extended period of time.	
Opportunity to choose child-initiated, adult-guided activities in the indoor or outdoor learning environment.		Access to the outdoor learning environment is limited.	
Time spent on activities appropriate to the developmental abilities of all boys, e.g. carpet time.		Boys are required to sit passively (on the carpet) for extended periods of time (over 15 minutes).	
Play is planned and supported by adults.		Play is not planned or supported by adults.	
Boys are given time to prepare for the next activity.		Boys are not given time to prepare for the next activity.	
Boys are given time to complete activity.		Boys are not given time to complete an activity.	

Boys Will Be Brilliant! published by Featherstone © Linda Tallent and Gary Wilson

The life cycle of a butterfly

Colour the pictures, then cut them out and stick them on the sheet in the right order

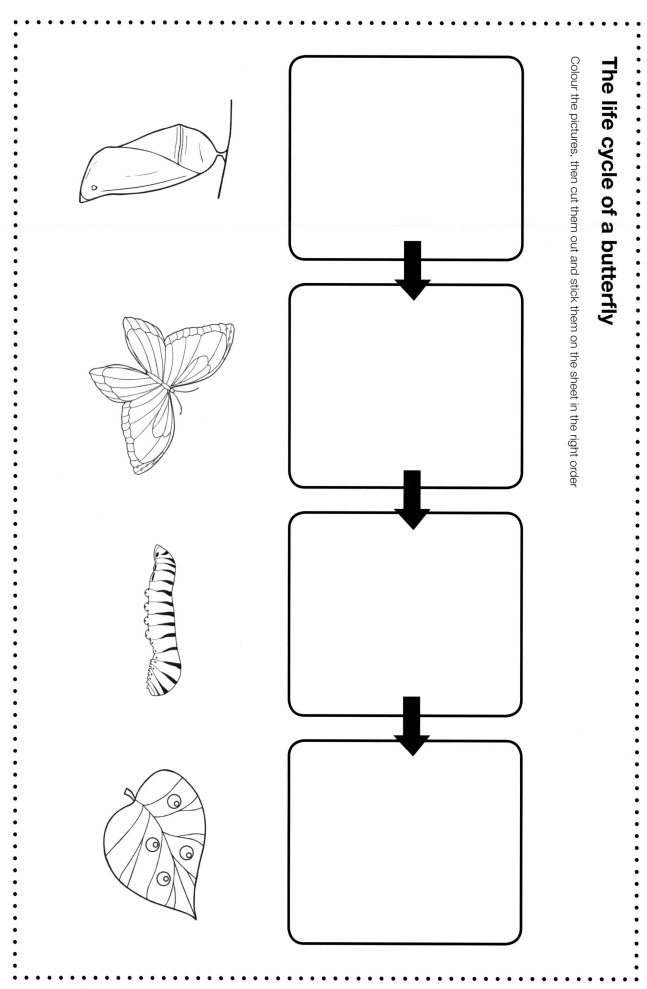

Maths around the home

Toy vehicles

- Sort them according to type, colour and size
- How many red, blue vehicles?
- Use a sheet of card to make a car park with numbered toys. Can you park the car in the correct bay?

Making biscuits

- Counting – how many spoonfuls of icing sugar/water have we used?
- How many eyes/noses?
- Can you cut the liquorice into 6 spikes for the hair?

Tidying the cupboards

- Sorting tins – how many altogether? How many more/less?

Setting the table

- How many people live in our house?
- How many spoons etc. do we need?
- Wonder how many taps/handles/steps/doors there are in our house?
- How many more doors than taps?

Garages

- Make garages using cardboard boxes. Park different numbers of cars in each garage. Use the language of more or less.
- Ask question, 'If I sell 3 cars, how many are left?'

Games

- Dominoes
- Dice games

Traditional play dough

- 1 cup flour

- 1 cup warm water

- 2 teaspoons cream of tartar

- 1 teaspoon oil

- ¼ cup salt

- food colouring

Mix all ingredients, adding food colouring last. Stir over medium heat until smooth. Remove from pan and knead until blended smooth. Place in plastic bag or airtight container when cooled.

Boys Will Be Brilliant! published by Featherstone © Linda Tallent and Gary Wilson

Picture books

These all show males in a positive light

My brother Sammy – Becky Edwards and David Armitage

The magic bicycle – Berlie Doherty and Christian Birmingham

My friend whale – Simon James

Piggybook – Anthony Browne

Jim's lion – Russell Hoban

Peter's place – Sally Grindley and Michael Foreman

Willy the chimp series – Anthony Browne

The lost thing – Shaun Tan

Weslandia – Paul Fleischman

Ben's trumpet – Rachel Isodora

Little bear's granddad – Nigel Gray

So much – Trish Cooke

My dad – Anthony Browne

My dad is brilliant – Nick Butterworth

My friend Harry – Kim Lewis

Clever dad – Maddie Stewart

Rainy day – Emma Haughton

Muhamad's desert night – Cristina Kessler

The best toy – Sarah Nash and Pamela Venus

New baby – Valerie Bloom

Good-bye papa – Una Leavy

Hue boy – Rita Phillips Mitchell

Prince cinders – Babette Cole

Bet you can't! – Penny Dale

For every child – Caroline Ccastle and UNICEF

Jump! – Michelle Magorian

Gregory Cool – Caroline Binch

World team – Tim Vyner

The shepherd boy – Kim Lewis

I have feelings – Jane Novotny-Hunter

Dad and me series – Jan Ormerod

Look what I've got! – Anthony Browne

Cleversticks – Bernard Ashley

Way home – Libby Hathorn

No more kissing! – Emma Chichester Clark

The grandad tree – Trisha Cooke

Since dad left – Caroline Birch

Beetle boy – Laurence David and David Lawrence

Tough Boris – Mem Fox and Kathryn Brown

Wilfrid Gordon Mcdonald Partridge – Mem Fox and Julie Vivas

References

Baron-Cohen, S. (2003) *The Essential Difference: Men, Women and the Extreme Male Brain.* Penguin

Brody, L.R. and Hall J.A. (1993) 'Gender and Emotion' in M.Lewis and J.M. Haviland (eds) *Handbook of Emotions.* New York. Guilford Press

Dunn, O. (2005) *Fatherese.* Nursery World

Ginott, H.G.(1975) *Teacher and child.* Avon Books

Hughes, M. (2002) *Teaching and learning of foundation subjects, training materials.* London DFES

Inkpen, M. (2008) *Kipper's Toybox.* Hodder Children's Books

Jarman, E. (2009) *The Communication Friendly Spaces Approach: Improving Speaking, Listening, Emotional Well-Being and General Engagement.* Elizabeth Jarman Limited

Lerner Dr. H (1999) *The Mother Dance.* Thorsons

Maynard, T. (2002) *Boys and Literacy: Exploring the Issues.* London. Routledge Falmer

Mischel W., Ebbesen E.B., Zeiss A.R. Marshmallow research J Pers Soc Psychol. 1972 Feb;21(2):204-18. *Cognitive and attentional mechanisms in delay of gratification.*

Ouvry (2003:18). *Exercising Muscles and Minds: Outdoor play and the early years curriculum.* National Children's Bureau

Svaleryd in OECD, (2004) *Confident, Capable and Creative: supporting boys' achievements.* DCSF Publications 2007

The Millennium Cohort Study Children of the 21st Century (volume 2): the first five years, www.policypress.co.uk

Trivette C.M., Dunst C.J., Gorman E. *Effects of parent-mediated joint book reading on the early language development of toddlers and pre-schoolers.* Centre for Early Literacy Learning (CELL) Reviews 2010; 3(2):1-15.